Becoming Happy!
Lessons from Nature

Melody Cheal

Published in England
by GWiz Publishing
(A division of The GWiz Learning Partnership)
Oakhurst, Mardens Hill, Crowborough, E. Sussex. TN6 1XL
Tel (+44) 1892 309205

info@gwiztraining.com

www.gwiztraining.com

First published 2016.
10 9 8 7 6 5 4 3 2

ISBN: 978-0-9548800-7-1

Acknowledgements

My personal development story started when I was sixteen years old. I was fortunate enough to have an inspirational teacher at school. Her name was Liz Fletcher and she was the first person who saw me as someone with potential. She held a positive image of me and encouraged me to be the best version of myself. In truth, it took me another fourteen years to break free of the shackles of self-doubt and limitation, yet that first experience of being valued planted the seed that would grow.

This book is in thanks to her and other inspirational teachers across the world. Thank you Liz for being Brilliant and helping me to be Brilliant too.

If you are wondering why the word "Brilliant" is such a big part of this book let me tell you. My husband, Joe and I say "Be Brilliant" to one another every day, particularly if we are going off to do things on our own. It has become our catch phrase and a reminder that Brilliance shines within each and every one of us. Thank you Joe for being the Brilliant Co-Star in my life.

Don't thin[k]
you are...
Know you[r]
are....
Because
you are
Brilliant!

www.gwiznlp.com

Introduction

I decided to write this book and illustrate it with photographs in order to share something of myself and hopefully provide some inspiration for those looking for ways to feel happier and more fulfilled in their lives.

The images are all my own and are a result of a recent hobby. In terms of quality, some are better than others if you look at them objectively. I invite you to consider them a metaphor. How often do you criticise yourself for not being good enough or maybe project that judgement onto others. I am learning photography and improving with each lesson. I know that if my pictures are compared to that of my teacher there will be a difference. The standard of my images are separate to my worth as a human being. I have value and thoroughly enjoyed taking each and every photograph (even the out of focus ones!)

I hope you are beginning to get the idea. You are a truly wonderful, magnificent being. Have you realised that yet?

The pages that follow include some ideas and tips on how to step into your magnificence and allow yourself to be the happy, joyous being you were always meant to be.

You are brilliant!

Let your brilliance unfold naturally, open up and be the best version of yourself.

www.gwiznlp.com

On Being Brilliant!

I wonder if you know what it means to be brilliant. My husband, Joe and I have been married for over twenty years and whenever one of us is heading out into the world we have a phrase we exchange:

Be Brilliant!

The phrase evolved naturally over time. It is a reminder that inside each and every one of us there is the potential to shine. If you have any doubt consider this: you are made up of the stuff of stars!

Every single atom that exists was once part of a star and as the universe unfolded, this stardust was transformed into a multitude of infinite variety of forms.

Take a moment to recognise who you really are: a being of infinite potential.

As you read this, notice any resistance within. What are you saying to yourself? What images do you see? For some of you there will be confirmation of your brilliance and for others perhaps you are learning something.

I haven't always recognised my own brilliance; I spent the first twenty nine years of my life living in the shadows. I was unhappy for much of the time and didn't really know why. Sometimes we need somebody else to switch on the light and help us wake up.

Are you ready?

We are all born beautiful, even Swans.

www.gwiznlp.com

Finding Beauty

External appearance is highly prized in modern society often in a sadly shallow and hollow way. Movie stars and models are paraded before us with digitally enhanced images creating an unrealistic standard.

Step back from all that and notice how human beauty is often based on fashion. Fashionable body shape, for instance, varies across decades, centuries and cultures. Some people have body shapes that naturally fit the current style while most of us are variations. So forget fashion!

What would happen if you just accepted that you are like a swan? You are beautiful and you deserve to feel good about yourself.

Feeling good about yourself comes from self-acceptance, self-respect and love. You need to find the beauty inside no matter how beautiful you are on the outside. This type of beauty shines out of your eyes creating a "magnetic field" that is more than skin deep.

www.gwiznlp.com

So how do you find beauty within yourself?

Start by knowing that when you are beautiful on the inside, others find you attractive. Your thoughts shape your internal landscape. Prune the thoughts that create ugly lines and nurture positive, warm reflections.

When you make a point of finding beauty in others you become less concerned with shallow outcomes. Each person has a unique and personal beauty that you will see if you provide a space free from judgement, allowing others to shine through their disguises.

Take care of your body and by all means take care of your appearance. There is an element of self-respect that comes from looking after yourself. Become a role model by treasuring your body, your face and the most beautiful feature of all, your smile.

Be Brilliant Today!
Shine on in every way!

www.gwiznlp.com

The Transformation Process

If you are like me, you may have found life a struggle at times. Perhaps you have not felt good about yourself. We are all a product of our early experiences and not everyone has a nurturing childhood to draw on.

I grew up with very low self-esteem and poor self-image. I felt unhappy much of the time. What sustained me during that time was the joy given to me by my dogs and nature. This book shares some of that joy with you and some of the things I have used to help me realise that I do have worth and value as do you.

Over the next few pages I will share with you some ideas to help you make a personal transformation... if you are ready to become the best version of yourself.

First idea:

You are already brilliant
and
the best version of you.

No-one else
is better at being you.

You are brilliant!

Taking Responsibility

Make a decision right now to take responsibility for your life and your happiness. You, and only you, can power your personal transformation. It is time to release the past and get back into the driving seat of your life.

When you take responsibility for yourself, you will step into your power. Start by reflecting on your history. Are you ruled by your history? Are you blocking yourself from good things because of fear, anger or faulty thinking?

I know this was true for me. So here are some ideas to start taking your life back. Start by focusing on a different aspect of your past; instead of focusing on pain, anger or fear, focus on strengths. What strengths do you have as a result of your history?

Write each strength down in your journal and include a description of what makes this strength special. Now write down at least three ways you can use this strength to improve your own life and that of others.

Find an image to represent each of these strengths and make a collage to inspire you to use these strengths every day.

Build a Team

One of the most important lessons for me was the discovery that I didn't need to do it alone! We are by nature a social animal and we thrive when we are surrounded by people who care for us.

The people you reach out to for help and support make a significant difference. Start by appreciating any positive, supportive cheerleaders that are already in your life.

Think carefully: who are the people who say and do things that boost you and leave you feeling better about yourself? Make a point of spending more time with these bright lights in your life.

On the other hand, who are the people that leave you feeling drained? If those draining you are family or friends that you want to keep in your life make a note. You will need to learn how to protect yourself from their negative energy.

There may be some people you need to gently move away from because their influence is unhealthy.

Consider finding some professional members for your team. I know that I certainly benefitted from seeking out counsellors, coaches and therapists to help me. Make sure you find someone who allows you to blossom.

Seek out new groups to join, filled with like-minded people who will raise you further.

www.gwiznlp.com

You are
accepted and loved.

Gaining New Perspectives

Do you see yourself as an optimist or a pessimist? I could talk about the glass being half-full but then again, had you realised that you can also re-fill a glass?

The mind-set you adopt will have a major impact on your general sense of well-being and it is a choice. This may come as a surprise to you.

What is a mind-set?

There are several components involved and each interacts with the other, creating our gestalt mind-set. Thoughts are often expressed as internal dialogue or self-talk. Sometimes you will be aware of this self-talk and you may have noticed that it can vary from positive, neutral or negative. At other times the dialogue is running almost as a background programme, reinforcing the beliefs and generalisations that you hold about yourself.

Some of these will be useful and others less so.

The second major component of mind-set is imagery and other sensory internal representations. We all carry around images, sound tracks and sensations based on experience and memory. We can also create fantasy representations of future events that will either motivate or block us.

Our thoughts and internal representations combine to create our feelings, which in turn impact on our physiology or body language. We take all of this and use it to filter our experience of the world, gathering evidence to support our perspective.

We ignore anything that would challenge our beliefs, generalisations and perceptions and if we can't ignore it, we change the meaning so that the result still confirms our mind-set. This is sometimes called the "self-fulfilling prophecy".

www.gwiznlp.com

Breaking the Cycle!

The first step is to recognise the cycle in the first place because self-awareness often precedes change. There are some steps you can take for yourself that will enhance your transformation.

Notice how you see yourself. Close your eyes and imagine an image of yourself. Do you see yourself as confident, capable and happy? How are you standing or sitting in that image? Are you animated or still? How do you feel about that image?

Make a few changes and notice how you feel as you do so. Start with the qualities of the picture, known as "sub-modalities" in NLP (Neuro-Linguistic Programming).

Make the picture colourful and vibrant... enlarge the image. Bring it a little closer and make the image sharp and focused.

Now change the content if necessary; make sure your posture is positive and confident. Notice your expression and if you are not looking happy, change the expression so that you are.

Notice how changing an internal image can change how you feel. There is more that you can do with this exercise if you understand the principles of NLP. If not, consider inviting an NLP Practitioner to join your professional support team

Changing Time

Temporal focus... where do you spend your time? The past, the present or the future?

Most people know the story of Scrooge and how he was shown the impact of his past and his present and what the future would hold as a result. On the strength of this, he changed his whole life script overnight. What a clever metaphor.

What if there was a way you could do a similar thing to transform your own life. How useful would that be for you?

In short, there is value in looking back at your history, value in experiencing life in the now and value in looking to the future. There are, however, positive ways of doing this and less than positive ways.

Notice where you spend your time. Do you spend time chewing over the past, experiencing now or looking to the future? And whatever your preference, how is that working for you?

www.gwiznlp.com

Second idea:

You are

Capable

of

Change

Looking
Back

www.gwiznlp.com

Past Timing!

Do you live in the past harking back to old experiences? And if you do, are the majority positive or negative?

When I first joined my husband, Joe's family, I found one of the family dynamics puzzling. Regularly the family would start telling stories from the past. It was often the same stories and most were either sweet or funny.

My family dynamic really didn't work that way. Talking about the past was just not part of the family pattern except for one thing: My dad had a tendency to talk a lot about the war (as in WWII).

The way my in-laws spoke about the past seemed to be positive and left everyone in a good mood. Their focus was on nostalgia and family bonding.

I reflected a little on how I didn't do that and wondered how I recalled the past? I often have conversations with people about events from my own past that I just don't remember. This can be neutral or even positive events.

How did that happen?

I realise that as with so many things in life, early programming is a big part of experience. My mother has an automatic response to any bad experience that she still uses today:

'Put it all behind you and move on!'

This is a great instruction for amnesia! There is a hidden message in the way my mother says it... that is 'forget about it'. This has some value for survival and yet can create limitations.

So my original set up was either forget about it or re-live the negative. Not very healthy. Later, I will share some ways to create positive recall of your past and reduce negative recall.

To complete the story of my in-laws: I now join in! It is great fun. I can now tell stories about events I wasn't even present for! Weirdly I have also created internal images of those stories! I have added to the store of stories over the last twenty years and been present for many joint ones.

Look up
and
smile

www.gwiznlp.com

www.gwiznlp.com

Releasing the Past

I want to pause for a moment to talk about how to handle intruding memories from the past. Most people are familiar with the concept of Post-Traumatic Stress Disorder and you may even know that this can involve "flashbacks" and bad dreams. What many people are less aware of is the idea of Post Traumatic Growth.

When people experience PTG instead of the disabling impact of PTSD, they find a way to make meaning from their experience. This appears to help them move on and become stronger as a result of their experience.

NB: If you suspect you are experiencing PTSD please seek some professional support.

For people who are stuck in negative memories, with or without trauma, the route to moving forward is the same. You need to find a way to make meaning from your past so you can move on.

In NLP we often work with the presupposition that a person hangs onto an old memory, behaviour or feeling for a reason. For example, if someone has been hurt in a certain situation, they may hold onto that memory and keep re-visiting it in order to avoid experiencing the same hurt in the future.

NLP has a number of specific processes that can help the individual to process this past event in a way that allows them to make meaning, whilst preserving the learning and reducing the emotional content. The result will be to move the prominence of the memory so that it becomes faded and less clear, while retaining the knowledge of the event.

Recent research has suggested that when people write things down about a past negative event, it can help them dissociate from the feelings.

Using this research and combining with NLP concepts, here is an exercise you could use if you need it.

1. Write down the event as a story with yourself in the leading role but written as if observed from afar.

2. Write down what the "star" of the story learnt from the experience, including important learnings about protecting themselves and staying safe. Perhaps about decision making or reaching out for help.

3. If there are other people involved in the story, write letters to each of them expressing any important emotions or opinions. Now burn the letters! This is important as it is part of the letting go.

4. Re-write the story with a different, more positive ending where either the "star" did something different or an appropriate co-star entered the scene to "save them".

5. Now go and do something just for fun that you really enjoy, preferably with people you care about.

How to remember the good old times!

Switching perspectives

When I first joined the Cheal clan I was very puzzled by their repeated story telling about the past. I even found myself becoming bored and thinking to myself 'here we go again!' I could have stayed with that attitude and completely missed the point but luckily I started to change.

Joe and I began having stories of our own. Joe would remind me of things like when we first met and fell in love. I found it very easy to engage in these stories because I was in them. I started to be the one to say "do you remember…."

In our relationship I realised that this is one of the mechanisms that has created the amazing relationship that we have. We constantly remember good experiences we have shared, as well as regularly adding new ones.

When we align to our values
we glide through life,
Finding someone to glide
with is a bonus.

www.gwiznlp.com

I often use this idea when working with people who want to bring the sparkle back into their lives. I recently did this in a demonstration on one of my workshops, NLP Practitioner. The delegate wanted to let go of feelings of irritation about her partner over a particular habit.

I asked the woman to tell me about when she first met her partner. She began to describe the first time she saw him. As she spoke her body language changed, her expression brightened and her skin took on a flush. I encouraged her to go over the story many times and with each repetition her feelings of love intensified. When I asked her to think about her husband's irritating habit in the light of that love, it no longer seemed important.

Deliberately re-living past experiences, both on your own but particularly with others, helps you stay in touch with those positive feelings. The mechanism is exactly the same as the one some people use to stay attached to a negative past.

I believe story telling out loud is more effective than writing down for this. The element of sharing the story is important too. This technique can be used by couples, families, friends and even in the work place to build team spirit.

My challenge to you is to build a positive reminiscence and share it with as many people as possible. I predict an increase in happiness!

Now is all there is!

Are you plugged in?

Our well-being benefits from the regular practice of meditation, mindfulness and connecting with the present moment. This needs to be balanced with learning from the past and planning for the future to create a rounded life. Being "present in the moment" sounds easy but is it?

Have you ever found yourself in the middle of an amazing experience and instead of just enjoying it, you begin thinking about how you are going to tell someone else about it! Or even worse you are pre-occupied with something else so don't notice what is happening to you. Sometimes we even find ourselves in a wonderful, peaceful moment only to get distracted by thoughts that are trivial and unimportant

If you read about living in the "now", you will be encouraged to focus purely on your sensory world in the here and now. What can you see, hear, feel, experience? What tactile sensations are you noticing? Your thoughts are about being. For many of us this is challenging. We might start evaluating our experience or thinking about someone we intend to share it with later. As a species we are easily distracted and maybe we are just in denial when we talk about having the attention span of a goldfish (as if that is not normal for human beings).

Interestingly enough, the place I find it easiest to be in the now is watching my fish in the pond. I find I can look at the fish and watch them swim round, distracting thoughts disappear and I relax fully. For me this is a form of meditation. The practice of mediation and the practice of mindfulness are two ways we can learn to stop our busy, hurry-hurry lives in order to recharge our batteries.

Many people have a perception of living in the now as being about peaceful stillness and communing with nature... developing a sense of serenity and well-being.

Practicing mindfulness is not really just about feeling relaxed and at peace. We can be present and totally focused on doing a mundane task or even challenging experiences. This can allow us to access peace and acceptance.

www.gwiznlp.com

Take a moment right now to stop and take ten full, deep breaths in and out. Focus fully on your body and how it feels to follow your breath all the way in and all the way out.

Did you stop? Did you focus on the now?

If the answer is 'no' stop reading and do it now...

Serenity is a choice, decide today

www.gwiznlp.com

Being in flow, how to get the most out of life

Recently I had a wonderful holiday on the Isle of Wight. The weather was amazing and we were spending our time with Joe's family. We all got on great and had a great experience.

The highlight for me came when I decided to set myself the goal of photographing some red squirrels in the wild. This shy creature is very rare in the UK and it is a privilege to see one.

I did my homework and some research. I contacted the Wight Squirrel Project. They very kindly told me about a hide on a reserve, where I had a good chance of seeing squirrels if I got up at dawn and took some walnuts with me. She advised me to put some walnuts where I wanted to take pictures.

So I got up at the crack of dawn and left Joe snoozing away. The dogs were a bit miffed at being left behind but went right back to bed as soon as I left!

I arrived at the hide and confess I was thinking this was going to be difficult. I had assumed I would need to put the nuts out some distance away and use my 500mm lens. But it seemed the hide was set up to look at the wet lands and I thought:

"Great,get up at dawn and nothing!"

www.gwiznlp.com

I started unpacking my camera gear anyway and then I heard it! The patter of tiny feet on the roof of the hide. The next thing I knew there was a squirrel two feet away from me demanding some food!

Well I had to change to a shorter lens!

It was then I entered the flow state. I lost all sense of time and found myself totally engrossed in what I was doing. Time passed without me noticing and I took picture after picture. It was amazing.

This for me is what "flow" is all about. Flow is not about "trying", flow emerges when we give ourselves up to a task or an experience. Any thoughts are about the here and now. We are fully engaged and time passes without us even realising it.

Make sure you give yourself permission to find what engrosses you and you will be able to find more joy.

Back to the Future!

What you focus on is what you get!

I wonder how you think about the future. Do you focus on what is possible or what might go wrong? The habit of imagining what might go wrong is called "catastrophizing".

There are varying degrees of catastrophizing. As with most psychological patterns there may well be a sliding scale, with one end extreme catastrophizing through to extreme "Polly Anna" focus. For Polly Anna there is only ever a positive outcome.

Both extremes can be unhelpful and finding a balance is key. As you learn to manage how you think about the future you will unlock the door to opportunity.

Breaking habitual patterns of thinking

The first step in all personal development is self-awareness. You cannot change anything unless you first notice and then acknowledge it.

The next step is to recognise that any habitual behaviour you have will have been formed originally for good reason. In NLP this is called the "positive intention" of the behaviour or thinking pattern.

This is based on the idea that you develop behaviours and patterns that help you survive in the world. Sometimes these are based on faulty logic because you lack all the relevant information and perspectives. The bottom line is: you do the best you can with what is available to you.

I mention this because it is vital that you give yourself a break and avoid beating yourself up over a historical thinking pattern. You need to forgive yourself and accept the behaviour for what it is, a habit.

Start to become mindful and notice the thought as it happens. Each and every time you notice negative future thinking use the following to stop yourself.

When opportunity
knocks make sure
you answer the door!

www.gwiznlp.com

1. Ask yourself: 'does this thinking have any basis in reality?' In other words do you need to do something?

2. If the answer to the above question was 'yes', take some appropriate action e.g. remove yourself from a situation that is unpleasant.

3. Having done the above or if the answer is 'no', make a conscious point of asking yourself: 'what are three great things in my life right now and three things in the near future I will enjoy?'

This technique is very much a cognitive technique requiring conscious thought but it can be very effective. There are other approaches to change thinking patterns including many within NLP. If you find the above is not working for you it might be worth investigating some alternatives with a qualified NLP Practitioner.

You are the most
perfect version of yourself.
Have you noticed?

www.gwiznlp.com

Daydreaming without a safety net

Still with the focus on the future, consider how you might live in the future in a positive way. Most people daydream. What kind of daydreams do you have?

For some it is about winning the lottery, meeting that perfect partner or making it as a movie star.

Generally you could argue this is a harmless pastime, a little bit of fun perhaps. Unfortunately for some the impact of this kind of daydreaming is far from harmless.

It can be the beginning of a hope/disillusionment cycle. Take the lottery as an example. The person imagines they have won the lottery and all the changes this will make in their life. They make the dream compelling, colourful and attractive adding layer upon layer of detail.

Lottery numbers are drawn and no matches. Disappointment!

This kind of daydreaming can become a form of disengagement with reality, leading to hopelessness and depression. In many ways it is a form of defence but can lead to unhappiness and lethargy in the long run.

I'm not saying give up daydreaming; a little "Walter Mitty" is good for us all but to pin your hopes on a fantasy can lead to disaster. It is not enough to just think positive thoughts. We need to do more and learn how to daydream constructively.

Constructive Daydreaming,

Bringing the future to life

So what is constructive daydreaming?

Here's my definition: taking yourself into the future in a way that is helpful and meaningful.

For example, last year we had some building work to improve the house. The work was major structural changes to our bedroom level. It is easy to see that with a project like this there was some planning involved!

We had been in this house for about eighteen months.

The bedroom level had four bedrooms but only one was a reasonable size. A whole one third of the floor space was a balcony. Although the views were and are stunning, the use of space was less stunning.

So we started to dream about how we would like things to be. In our imagination we created a layout and design. We imagined having all the space we could desire. Anyone who has ever been involved in building work will know dreaming is not enough. We had to get planning permission, work out how we would pay for it and then find a trustworthy builder to do the work.

This is all very practical, however in order to do this we need to put ourselves into the future and look back to see the end result. In NLP we call this "future pacing". When we do this with practical projects it can sometimes help us to check out if we even really want the change. Future pacing is also important with less tangible goals too. For example making a major life change or finding a relationship.

www.gwiznlp.com

What you focus on is what you get!

When I first started working with people as a counsellor and more recently a coach, I noticed that often my clients would have a really long list of things they didn't want.

For example, a single woman wanting a relationship would tell me all about the type of man she did not want to have a relationship with. She would be able to tell me in great detail about the personality, habits and even appearance of the man she under no circumstances wanted to meet.

What happened next?

She would come to sessions telling me how she kept meeting people who fit her description but nothing else. This is creating your own reality in action. Was she really creating these men? Of course not but she was giving her unconscious mind instructions about what to look out for.

Try this experiment right now. Look around the room you are in and notice anything that is "Red".

Now close your eyes and ask yourself "what in this room is green". Open your eyes and check. How much did you miss?

Our minds need direction on what to pay attention to and if we tell ourselves to ignore something, we are merely highlighting the very thing we don't want. For example, whatever you do right now do not think about chocolate.

Rapport is a beautiful thing.

Who do you need to be more connected to?

www.gwiznlp.com

What happened?

So what do we need to do instead? For people looking for a relationship I give a task.

Write down on at least four sides of paper, in detail, what you would like in a partner. This focuses the mind on the right things and you are more likely to meet that person.

Be ready because you never know when your next adventure begins

Preparing for Future Adventures

Imagine that you have a goal you wish to achieve in the future. The idea is to make that imagined outcome as detailed as possible. See yourself as you will be in the future having achieved the goal. See what is different in your life as a result. Listen to what you can hear in the future experience, including what you are saying yourself, what you can hear around you and even what you are telling yourself internally.

Fully experience that future as if you have stepped into that version of yourself and you can now feel exactly what it feels like to have achieved that goal. Bring all of that feeling back with you to motivate you in taking the next smallest step needed to achieve the goal. Repeat this process until you get there.

Sometimes when you do this, you will realise that the goal is not what you wanted after all and at other times you will get confirmation that you are on the right track.

You can also use this technique if you want to stop a behaviour. I'll use the example of eating unhealthily. Before eating the food that in the present moment you may be craving, imagine you have already eaten it... take yourself to several hours later.

How does your body feel, what are you saying to yourself? Do you have regrets?

Often this can be enough to allow you to make a healthier choice. You can do this with more complex issues around relationships, jobs, moving house etc.

Using Mental Rehearsal to

Create your Future

So firstly a definition: mental rehearsal is the act of imagining yourself in a situation you normally find challenging and seeing yourself being successful.

Earlier I mentioned the negative version of mental rehearsal known as "catastrophising". In catastrophising you imagine everything that could possible go wrong – the fantasies are endless. The amazing thing is, sometimes the really "off the wall" things you worry about actually happen. This is the power of mental rehearsal; it is as if you become a magnet for the experiences you imagine.

How much more powerful if you focus on positive outcomes!

Let your creativity run free!

Dream and
let your ideas
take flight

www.gwiznlp.com

Before I discuss how to do this, let me give you some of the background... and we need to start by looking at how the brain works. Whenever we go into any situation, our brain triggers what is known as a generalised memory. This generalised memory is sub-conscious and gives us unconscious messages about how to behave, think and feel in the situation.

This generalised memory is the amalgamation and edited experiences from your past relating to a particular type of situation. The generalised memory has neural pathways connected to a number of different "anchors" or stimuli. When an anchor is triggered the programme runs. For instance, you may have a particular programme that runs when faced with conflict; it may vary according to gender, age or status of the other person resulting in "knee jerk" reactions. Some knee jerk reactions are positive in which case I would advise you to leave them alone but others can be really unhelpful.

Mental rehearsal allows you to invent your own generalised memory to replace the old programme. It is replaced using constant repetition making the pathway to the new memory stronger than the pathway to the old one.

Mental Rehearsal Exercise

Close your eyes.

Imagine yourself in the situation in as much detail as possible.

Imagine everything happening the way you would like it to.

See yourself easily and effortlessly, overcoming any barriers or obstacles that may arise. This is vital, if you miss this stage out you may get thrown when obstacles appear in real life.

Imagine the situation coming to a successful and satisfying conclusion.

End by imagining some form of celebration or appreciation of your success. Get really silly with this and have some fun. The idea here is to intensify the positive experience and anchor it into the brain.

Finding purpose, following your mission

A topic often discussed in Positive Psychology is that of meaning. When we have meaning and purpose in our lives we tend to be happier. If we can find meaning out of obstacles and even tragedy, we recover quicker.

Finding your life purpose can help you focus and create a sense of direction. This direction can help you recognise the contribution you are making to the world. When you feel a sense of contribution, you feel more connected to others and your levels of happiness are likely to increase.

Double the curiosity
and you
double the learning!

www.gwiznlp.com

Get Curious!

What could your purpose be? There are no rules and your contribution can be very private or can be more "out there". For example, you could focus on being the best parent you can be or perhaps contribute by inventing gadgets that make life easier. Maybe you make your garden a nature reserve or you put effort into conserving energy to help the planet.

On our NLP Master Practitioner programme we have a guided hypnosis session to allow our students to connect with their personal mission. You could use a similar approach to discover your own purpose or you could just decide.

Change your perception and notice your whole reality shift

www.gwiznlp.com

Getting perspective,

How am I creating this?

I want to introduce you to an idea that can set you free. The template I offer comes from NLP and involves how we can move from being "at effect" to "at cause" in our life. When we are "at effect" there is a feeling of helplessness and we feel victim like. Being "at cause" is when we have reclaimed our power and taken responsibility for the future.

When I first began my own personal development journey, over twenty years ago the following idea helped me to recondition my own responses.

Whenever I found myself in a situation where I felt helpless or hard done by I would ask myself a question:

'How am I creating this?'

Now for those of you who have seen the movie, "The Matrix", you may well think I am heading there, and in a way I am. But only in a way. I'm not suggesting that we are all plugged into a computer, however what if we were clouding our perceptions based on faulty thinking.

We are not responsible for the actions of others, however sometimes we may be allowing or even encouraging behaviours in others that may be leaving us feeling victim like. We may be getting ourselves into difficult situations because we are not well informed or because we set ourselves up for problems. All of this results from how we interact with the world and this is something we do have control over.

When others treat you badly or take advantage of you, it is worth considering what you are doing that gives that person permission to do that? In his book Life Strategies, Dr Phil McGraw describes what he calls the ten Life Laws and number 8 is particularly relevant with regard to the above:

'We teach others how to treat us.'

If we accept this as true, it allows us to review our interactions in a new and more empowering way because here is the really good news! We are likely to get the opportunity to "do over". What does that mean, I hear you say!

We all recreate repeating cycles of behaviour and experience. As we do this we attract people into our lives who know how to deliver what we expect to receive. You will in some way be fulfilling a pattern of theirs too.

My challenge to you is to identify the repeating patterns of behaviour in your life and having identified them start the process of change.

If you realise you are banging your head
against a brick wall, stop and do
something else.

www.gwiznlp.com

www.gwiznlp.com

Becoming Magnificent!

The Resilient Mind.

In their book "The Power of Resilience", Robert Brooks and Sam Goldstein suggest that in order to build a resilient mind we need to 'feel special'.

Before I add my thoughts, I need to clarify what this means. Being special is about recognising your own value and worth as a human being, it is not about being self-centred. This distinction is essential; without it there is a risk that we act as if we are entitled to certain outcomes, experiences and material things.

This is something that happened when there was a concerted effort to increase self-esteem in children in the States several decades ago. Children were told how wonderful and awesome they were but were not given sufficient boundaries and responsibilities. This resulted in a whole generation of young adults with an entitlement attitude, many of them did not work but expected their parents to still be providing for them aged 30 years and more.

Most modern programmes aimed at helping children develop healthy self-esteem and resilience incorporate boundaries and the development of values such as consideration, responsibility and compassion. They also foster the importance of feeling special.

This step was a major one for me. I grew up with very low self-esteem and very little emotional resilience. I did not believe myself to be special and failed to recognise my own value or that of others. I was in a very bitter and unhappy place. For me, the turning point was the sudden realisation that I had as much right as anyone else to lead a happy life and that I did have many positive qualities. I was able to accept that I was loveable and likeable, something that I had not believed before this.

www.gwiznlp.com

Spread your wings and fly, let your dreams take shape

Third idea:

You are whole and resourceful.

You have all the resources you need.

You are capable of change.

Choice always exists.

www.gwiznlp.com

How can you get to feel special?

The first step is to reach out. As I have mentioned earlier, I believe that we are most successful at personal development when we engage with others. We need to be in the company of people who already have that feeling of being special and who are willing to support you in making your transformation. We are social animals and sometimes we need to see our own magnificence reflected back to us in the mirror of another being.

When did you decide you were anything less than magnificent? Are you ready to re-discover your own dazzling brilliance? As a place to start, consider a few startling facts about you as a human being;

www.gwiznlp.com

1. You have a body that is keeping you alive automatically. It breathes, your heart beats, your organs do amazing work. Are you taking care of your body?

2. You have a brain that is processing millions of bits of information and sending signals to your body to take action. I wonder if you are appreciating how magnificent your brain is.

3. You have emotions that enable you to connect with   others and to feel joy, pain, pleasure, compassion,   sadness, anger and more. These emotions help you make sense of the emotional world... do you listen to your emotions?

4. And if all that is not enough, every atom in your body was once the centre of a star! You are literally a star and you are special! Are you ready to accept that yet?

For many of us we need help getting there. We need to deal with our baggage, old limiting beliefs and negative internal dialogue that has been keeping us stuck. Reach out as that first step, realising already that you are special even if you have not yet allowed yourself to feel it. The first step begins the journey.

www.gwiznlp.com

www.gwiznlp.com

Becoming Wise,

The reward for getting older

Finally, I thought it would be good to consider the good things that come with getting older. In modern society there is often a focus on the young and staying youthful, as if aging is in some way wrong. What a shame that so many people become anxious about this natural progression.

In more ancient societies, age and wisdom were prized and the various phases of our life each had a value. In my studies of Positive Psychology and Wisdom at university, the following points were presented:

There is a rich repertoire of "procedural" knowledge, the know-how to perform certain skills such as complex decision making about interpersonal problems and conflict resolution.

Wisdom is the ability to appreciate the many themes and contexts in life such as family, self, community, culture and the inter-relations across a life span.

It also brings tolerance for differences in values and priorities. The wise person is respectful of the unique set of values an individual holds, even if they differ from their own.

And with wisdom we are more able to handle ambiguity and uncertainty. We recognise that with regard to the past and the present while uncertain about the future. All of this is taken into account when solving problems.

Perhaps most interesting of all during my studies was the fact that wisdom is not guaranteed as we get older, we need to be open to it. Also there are wise young people too.

Are you allowing yourself

to embrace your

potential for wisdom?

Are you letting go of

superficial judgements

encouraged by society?

Are you ready to be wise enough

to be happy

just as you are?

Be who you were meant to be, your purpose will become clear.

www.gwiznlp.com

If you would like help in your journey from me, reach out to me. I want to help you. If you are local enough or can travel, I'd love to see you on one of my workshops or for one-to-one support. If travel is challenging, still contact me as I have a wide network across the world and I may be able to put you in touch with someone who lives nearer to you.

Contact me via my website

www.gwiznlp.com

Fourth idea:

"No matter what
you think you are,
you are always
and in all ways
more than that!"

Julie Silverthorn

About the Author

Melody lives on the edge of Ashdown Forest, East Sussex with her husband, Joe and two dogs, Buck and Remus. She has a degree in Psychology, an MSc in Applied Positive Psychology, a diploma in Psychotherapy and is an NLP Master Practitioner and Certified NLP Master Trainer. She is part of the external verification panel for the ANLP accreditation programme. Her Psychological Approaches to Coaching Diploma is accredited by the Association for Coaching.

She regularly speaks at national conferences and has presented her dissertation research, 'NLP and self-esteem', at an international research conference. Her work was published in an academic journal as a result. She is also the co-author of the popular book, 'The Model Presenter'.

Contact Melody via her website www.GWizNLP.com

Lightning Source UK Ltd.
Milton Keynes UK
UKIC03n2322120416
272134UK00005B/9